PATHWAYS TO CHURCH GROWTH

THE FIRST YEAR

Incorporating New Members

SUZANNE G. BRADEN

D1566131

DISCIPLESHIP RESOURCES
MATERIALS FOR GROWTH IN CHRISTIAN FAITH AND LIFE
P.O. Box 189 • Nashville. TN 37202 • Phone (615) 340-7284

PATHWAYS TO CHURCH GROWTH SERIES

Taking Attendance: Growing Through Worship, Hoyt L. Hickman

The First Year: Incorporating New Members, Suzanne G. Braden

Invite: Preaching for Response, O. Dean Martin

Worship and Evangelism, Andy Langford and Sally Overby Langford

Every Member in Ministry: Involving Laity and Inactives, John Ed Mathison

Pray and Grow: Evangelism Prayer Ministries, Terry Teykl

Personal Prayer-Evangelism Guide, Terry Teykl

Library of Congress Catalog Card No.: 86-72749

ISBN 0-88177-046-9

DR046B

CONTENTS

FOREWORD

United Methodist churches throughout the world are making covenants to grow in ministry and grow in numbers. We believe that church growth will come as a result of our witness and service in the world. We know that churches grow when Christians share their faith stories with persons who are alienated from God or who are not involved in the life of the church. We gain this perspective from reading scripture, from studying the conversion experiences of Christians through the centuries, and from our own personal experience.

We also know that as disciples we must receive new persons in our congregations and avoid judging their faith stories or dismissing their struggle to know God. Thus we help all persons relate to God and develop Christian faith, equipping them and sending them out as disciples of the One who is the Lord of all of life.

We can translate this evangelistic commission into the language of those who study the reasons for church growth. One fruitful way to describe the reasons for church growth is to identify 1) factors that attract persons to the gospel and the church, 2) factors that influence persons to make a commitment to Christ and membership in a congregation, and 3) factors that bond persons in their relationship with Christ and the church.

Each pastor and each lay minister of the gospel knows that there are no snappy solutions, no easy five or ten steps which should result in "x" number of persons attending Sunday morning worship. Yet we can identify factors that focus our prayer and ministry on the pathways to church growth. Pastors of growing churches prefer to rank the factors which contribute to membership growth. Our research shows that the top ten factors are:

1. Vital worship services
2. Fellowship and relational settings
3. Pastor and pastoral functions
4. Sharply targeted ministries

5. Community/world   8. Physical facilities and
   Outreach   location
6. Christian education   9. Lay leadership/involvement
7. Growth posture/planning   10. Evangelism activities

   This series, Pathways to Church Growth, includes books and booklets containing practical suggestions for ministry related to these ten factors. The resources are written by leaders in the church and by successful pastors of growing churches. This book by Suzanne Braden discusses that crucial first year when over 50 percent of new members choose to fade from a commitment to their congregation. Suzanne gives fresh suggestions on how to incorporate new persons into the life of your congregation.
   I invite you to join together with Christians everywhere in redoubling your ministry and commitment to a growing church. Tell your story about what God has done for you, and encourage people in your community who want to know how Christ makes a difference in our lives.

EZRA EARL JONES
General Secretary
General Board of Discipleship
The United Methodist Church

INTRODUCTION

Observers of congregational life in the United States are estimating that over one half of the adults who join mainline Christian churches drop into inactivity in their first year of membership. Many more new members fail to become actively involved in the life and ministry of their congregations.

This situation is not inevitable. Congregations can understand themselves better; they can develop more sensitivity to the hopes and needs of new members; they can organize and manage ministries that invite people into deeper faith and broader participation in congregational life.

The process of helping new members find places of belonging and service in a congregation is often labeled "assimilating" new members. In this booklet, the word *incorporation* will be used throughout instead of the word *assimilation*.

In the United States there is, in many places, strong pride in one's ethnic roots. For many the word *assimilation* implies the image of a melting pot, in which everyone gets blended into the whole until everyone looks, thinks, and acts the same. People with ethnic pride do not want to be melted down to look like everyone else. In truth, surely all of us want to retain our individuality to some degree. We want to be a part of the larger group; we want to make our own contributions.

It seems appropriate to use the Apostle Paul's image of the church as the Body of Christ and to talk of helping new members become part of this living Body. Thus we talk about the incorporation of new members into/onto the Body of Christ, the church.

When we think of our congregations as the Body of Christ, and when we talk of incorporating new members, we are reminded that we are not all alike, that we have been given different gifts, different parts in order to function more completely. New members, even those who seem very unlike us, bring unique gifts or fresh commitments which are always important to our congregation's function as the Body of Christ in the whole world. Moreover, the images surrounding the word *incorporation* remind us of our responsibility to help newcomers discover which part of the Body of Christ they are or can be.

When we begin to talk and to think about the incorporation of new members into the life and ministry of God's church, we are straining to understand what our brothers and sisters are looking for and responding to; we sinful human beings are pushing ourselves and our congregations to be open to strangers, even those we fear or those with whom we feel little sympathy or connection.

The incorporation of new members is a difficult task. But it is important work for the new members and for our congregations, because seriousness about incorporating new members leads congregations to ask: Who are we? (If we consider ourselves called by God to be the church, does that mean we must assume that new members are being called by God also?) Why do we (this congregation, this denomination) do what we do? What does it mean to be a member? How might God want to use this particular congregation, this particular Body of Christ?

If these questions are considered thoughtfully, prayerfully, and deeply, they can open doors to a new sense of spiritual vitality and missional purpose.

In Part One we will consider some of the basic needs of newcomers to our congregations. We will pay attention to how paths into the heart of congregational life differ in some ways according to the size of the congregation. In Part Two we will look at seven specific strategies that congregations can implement immediately as they build their own pathways to church growth. Our focus will be on that crucial first year of membership.

Getting Started

1. Read through the first three chapters of this guide.
2. Have one or more of the task force report their evaluation of your congregation using the appropriate chart in Chapter Two. Discuss.
3. Have one or more members of the task force fill in the chart at the end of Chapter Three and report their assessment and recommendations. Discuss.
4. Evaluate your response to the questions for an Incorporation Committee and the responses made to the New Member Survey.
5. Choose strategies and make recommendations to your Administrative Council or Board.

Part One

INCORPORATING NEW MEMBERS

1. PROFILES AND PREDICTIONS

Sarah Houseman has been a member of Good Neighbor Christian Church for a year. She automatically joined Good Neighbor Church when she married Ben and returned to his family's farm. Ben's family has farmed this land for five generations, and for most of those years they have been pillars of the community and leaders in the church.

During their courting years in college, Sarah often heard Ben speak of Good Neighbor Church with affection and appreciation for how the church helped him feel closer to God. Although Sarah did not grow up as a churchgoer, she looked forward to being a part of Good Neighbor Church.

Unfortunately, life isn't going the way Sarah expected. Unlike Ben, she doesn't feel surrounded and supported by happy loving aunts, uncles, and cousins. Church activities don't seem like family gatherings to Sarah; in fact, she usually feels left out or invisible at church. The forty or fifty people who participate in all church functions are polite and kindly, but they are still treating her like a guest, and she often feels lost in the crowd. The women don't seem to need her help in the kitchen when there are meals to prepare or dishes and tables to clean.

The Sunday school classes, even the nursery class, have established and revered teachers. Sarah seldom understands what is being discussed. In worship, words and phrases are used in the sermons, prayers, and music that Sarah hasn't ever heard before. Since she doesn't want the other members to know that she didn't grow up in church, she doesn't ask for explanations. Even in the informal conversations Sarah often feels lost because she wasn't around when beloved Brother John was pastor or when the high school girl's basketball team beat that huge, city high school team to win the regional championship. Sarah never knew "Uncle" George Johnson who put the community on the map when he was in the state legislature, and she doesn't know much about farming, gardening, or putting up food for the winter. Sarah is discouraged and lonesome. The place where she usually feels worst is at church, so Sarah is beginning to make excuses so she won't have to attend all the functions which Ben and the rest of his family attend.

With her marriage, Sarah expected to become a part of two new families—Ben's immediate family and his church family. She assumed,

1

and perhaps everyone else has assumed, too, that her position as Ben's wife would give her an automatic place in the life of the congregation. They all are mistaken.

Sarah needs to know the people, the history, the faith story, and language of Good Neighbor Church. Good Neighbor Church needs to know Sarah's history and to recognize her pain and confusion. Until the congregation sees Sarah as an individual and is willing to adopt her into the church family, she will continue to feel like an invisible outsider.

*   *   *   *   *

Marian and Don Bergman retired last year from jobs each loved: Marian was the office manager of a growing company, and Don ran a community service project. They were tired of the winters in their northeastern city and now live six months of the year in a dynamic retirement area in a sunbelt city.

Marian's and Don's church "back home" was very important to them. That congregation supported and challenged them throughout their adult lives. In fact, Don left the business world to work with street people as a direct result of the faith challenges and support he and Marian experienced there. They do not intend to move their membership from that congregation, but they are eager to find a church home in their new winter location.

They thought that Sunshine Community Church might be the place for them. Its sanctuary reminded them of the one they feel so comfortable with at home; the congregation is about the same size as their other church; and the worship service is familiar and comforting. But lately they've begun to wonder if the Sunshine Church is what they are looking for. To be sure, the members are friendly and creative in their efforts to meet newcomers to their area.

The Bergmans first attended Sunshine Church because they saw the church's ad in the community newspaper which specifically invited people from Marian's and Don's home state to worship the next Sunday. It had been fun to see so many people from their state, and they felt comfortable and welcomed, so they kept coming back. The church is friendly and creative, and there is always something going on: potluck meals, bridge tournaments, quilting sessions, sightseeing trips, craft shows, gardening workshops—the list goes on and on. Marian and Don have enjoyed many of these activities and have made a lot of new friends, but the church feels more like a community center to them than church. They miss the serious Bible study at home, the Sunday school class that prays together and helps each other discover where God is leading them in their everyday lives. Most of all they are missing the relationship they have with the pastor at home. They understand that the pastor of the Sunshine Church has her hands full coordinating church activities, leading worship, and visiting the ill or bereaved. Nevertheless, they long for some serious Christian conversation and teaching.

Although Marian and Don want to continue seeing many of the people at Sunshine Church, they have been thinking about visiting some of the other churches in their new winter hometown.

Marian and Don, like most other people, expect to make new friends when they become a part of a congregation. They would be unlikely to remain in a congregation where they did not find friends. Nevertheless, in their search for a church home in their winter location, Marian and Don primarily are looking for a place where they can continue to explore seriously their relationship with God. They want to live in the ways God is calling them to live, and they want help in discerning what these ways may be.

They will continue to drop away from Sunshine Church until they see signs that Sunshine Church also is serious about helping them grow and live out their Christian commitments.

*   *   *   *   *

Paul Malone joined First United Methodist Church last year. The huge sanctuary, extraordinary choir, and worship service attracted him and at first made him feel less lonely in the city. Paul had been recently divorced and was determined to build a full new life for himself and his young son.

During the worship services, Paul notices a number of other people about his age, and some of them seem to be attending the service alone. He would like to meet some singles but never sees them at other church activities. In fact, Paul is having trouble developing friendships with the other people his age that he has met. He has tried several Sunday school classes and found only married couples there. It's still painful for Paul to realize that he is no longer part of a "couple." He is beginning to bring his son to Sunday school and then to walk down the block to drink coffee and read the Sunday paper until worship time.

Even Paul's son Jonathan doesn't seem to be making many friends at Sunday school. His class is quite large, with children from nine different schools in the city. Although there are two other children from Jonathan's school, they are not close friends of Jonathan's. Just like adults, the children often are so eager to see old friends that they tend to pay little attention to the newcomer. The children in Jonathan's Sunday school class are quite close due to a very active children's program which includes a choir and numerous creative weekday activities. Unfortunately, Jonathan and other children of single working parents rarely can participate because transportation cannot be provided by their parents. Paul wants Jonathan to participate, but simply cannot leave work at three o'clock once a week in order to get Jonathan to the church. He talked with one of the ministers about the situation and was asked to be part of the church's children's ministries task force, but the task force meets during the day when Paul cannot attend.

The situation is complicated because Jonathan spends some weekends and holidays with his mother who is not involved in any church life at all.

Paul himself longs for the support of some sort of church family, and he deeply wants Jonathan to grow up nurtured and challenged by the church. In fact, First Church's reputation as a dynamic "family" church with an impressive list of family activities was the deciding factor in Paul's decision to join First Church. Now he is beginning to feel as though "family" doesn't mean a single father and his son. He and Jonathan are finding it harder and harder to devote so much of their free time on Sunday to Sunday school and worship at First Church.

*   *   *   *   *

Mary and Byron Rowen are also fairly new members at First United Methodist. They joined about the same time as Paul Malone because they were also attracted by First United Methodist's reputation as a family church. But, unlike Paul, May and Byron almost immediately found happy Sunday school situations for themselves and for their three children. In fact, Mary and Byron liked the first class they tried so much that they never revisited any of the other adult classes. Several couples in that class have children the same ages as the Rowens, and are very involved in the children's ministries of First Church. They were quick to include the Rowens in various aspects of the children's ministry. Mary has already become part of the teaching team for the five-year-olds and Byron has agreed to work as a junior high counselor in the fall.

At first the Rowens were flattered that First Church seemed so eager for their input and help with the children and youth work, but now they are beginning to worry a bit that they have become too involved too quickly.

Mary is remembering that working with a large group of preschool children is not something she has ever enjoyed doing, and she wishes she had remembered that week of Vacation Bible School teaching several years ago that had been such a struggle for her. She was so pleased when First Church called on her that she accepted the children's job and forgot that she had just been thinking that she might enjoy working with some of the older members of this congregation.

Mary doesn't realize it, but Byron too is having second thoughts about working with the youth. His unspoken reason for joining First Church was to support Mary in getting the children settled in a program of Christian education. He wants to devote his energy to his new job and to making a place for himself in the business community of this new town. Byron knows he doesn't have time for the youth job, but when Jack called to recruit him, he couldn't say no. After all Jack has already introduced Byron to several important contacts and seems truly interested in helping Byron get established.

What had seemed like such a warm, welcoming church just a few months ago, is beginning to feel a little "pushy" to the Rowens. Nevertheless, they still are impressed by the programming and ministries of First Church, and they like what happens in the worship services. They do wish sometimes they knew a bit more about The United Methodist Church, such as its history and organization. This is the first United Methodist church they've attended, but they agreed before this move not to choose, this time, between Mary's Baptist tradition and Byron's Episcopal one. They haven't been too surprised by any United Methodist customs yet, but they think they would really enjoy some more specific instruction on being United Methodists.

In short, things aren't going badly for the Rowens at First Church, but, on the other hand, things aren't getting better there for them either. Both are hoping to make it through the next year.

                              *   *   *   *   *

Large membership churches like First Church often attract people by their wide range of quality programming. Nevertheless, sometimes people who remain impressed by the programming do drop out of these churches. Like Paul Malone, they do not find people with whom they can share their life and faith struggles. Surrounded by numbers of people, they are lonely and unable to make personal contact. They drop out.

Large membership churches with a number of programs and ministries need a lot of volunteer help to maintain the activities. They are tempted to focus on the jobs that need doing rather than on the gifts and needs of their members. Too often new members are recruited for jobs before serious efforts are made to help them discern where God is leading them. This can result in folks feeling like the Rowens—flattered but also pressured, a bit frustrated and misunderstood. They are likely candidates for burnout and inactivity.

*   *   *   *   *

Every church could uncover a story similar to one we've just read. And every church that wants to be serious about helping people develop as Christian disciples will ask itself what is happening to the people like Sarah, the Bergmans, Paul and Jonathan Malone, or the Rowens who have become involved in the life of its congregation.

What is likely to happen to the new member who is a middle-aged, never married man? What about the woman whose husband refuses to participate with her or to support her participation? What about the couple who is new to town and whose oldest child has periodic health crises? What about the shy teenager who joins only because his parents are joining? The list could go on and on, but the point, of course, is to urge all congregations to take a careful look at its new members and to consider carefully how the congregation can assist each new member to grow in his or her love of God and of neighbor.

Far too often, congregations fall into the trap of behaving as though they worked hard, and now the work is over when people decide to sign on as members. In fact, experience and statistics tell us that the congregation's responsibility is just beginning, and the congregation and the new member are both entering a crucial time in their life together. Some observers are convinced that if new members are not well incorporated into the life and ministry of the congregation within six months of joining, they are quite likely to drop out of active participation in church life.

Much has been written about the bonds that hold a person and a congregation together. These bonds develop, deepen, and change over time. The new member will not have the depth and breadth of relationship that longer term members have, but several points of contact seem to be most important. A well incorporated new member is likely to be described as a person who:

- Feels the congregation is helping him or her grow spiritually

- Has personal friends within the congregation
- Has identified a gift or calling and is exercising that gift or calling, perhaps through some job or leadership role in the congregation
- Understands, identifies with, and supports the history and current goals of the congregation
- Is involved in the worship life of the congregation
- Is excited about the congregation and naturally invites unchurched friends to participate in church activities

During a newcomer's first months of membership, the congregation must be intentional about helping the newcomer connect with these points of contact, points of bonding with the congregation.

Far too many people are expected to "sink or swim" on their own once they've joined our congregations. Far, far too many sink into inactivity. Indeed, some of them will be so badly disappointed by this church experience that they will be very resistant to invitations from other Christians and other congregations. Some may never risk participating in church life again.

Sometimes we are tempted to discuss the incorporation of new members into the life and ministry of the church from an institutional and functional perspective; i.e., how can we help these people become good, responsible members of our congregation? How can we prevent them from becoming inactive? We will do well to alter our attitude and hold always before ourselves the questions, How can our organization help these people see more clearly God's active presence in the world and in their lives? How can we help them claim and carry out the ministries to which God may be calling them? To be sure, churches with well-functioning, intentional programs for incorporating new members use the insights of those who study organizations and the methods by which organizations develop their members' loyal commitment and participation. The church is concerned about building good, responsible members, but our concern grows not from our institutional need but rather from our conviction that the church is Christ's primary means today of drawing people closer to God and to each other.

The purpose of this book is to help congregations think about the religious and social needs of their new members and to develop strategies for addressing those needs. The basic assumption of this book is that the church is called to make disciples, not merely productive church members. Or to say much the same thing in another way, we believe that the church exists to serve God and God's people, not to perpetuate itself. Our focus here will be on the Christian disciple, on his or her concerns, hopes, needs, and growth.

Our second assumption is that people join the church with sincerity and with the hope that their lives and their relationship with God will be strengthened. Studies show that many do not recognize or are unable to talk about this deep longing. People do say that they are joining because they want to be with friends, or because they want Christian education for their children, or because they think they will be more comfortable in a new community if they are part of a local congregation. In fact, the reasons given for joining a church may be as numerous and indi- vidualistic as the people joining.

However, it is our conviction that it is increasingly rare, if indeed it ever were the case, that people join the church purely as a matter of social convention. In almost every community today there are civic groups, social clubs, hobby and study groups, athletic teams, etc., through which people can meet their needs for fellowship, intellectual enrichment, and service. The church's distinctiveness is that only the church exists to help people relate more meaningfully to God and consequently to neighbor.

People join churches with hopes that their lives will be changed, that they can and will feel a closer connection to God, that God's meaning and purpose can be brought to bear on their own lives. Therefore, when we see in our own congregation a number of inactive members and when we read the predictions that well over one-half of those who join congrega- tions drop into inactivity quite soon after joining, we are alarmed. We are alarmed not because many people so quickly fail to support our churches as they have promised. We are alarmed because we fear our congregations have failed those who came to us with urgent, though perhaps inarticu- late, longings and high hopes.

2. SMALL, MEDIUM, OR LARGE

Finding a home in a congregation, discovering what part of the Body of Christ one is called to be, is a process that begins before newcomers first visit the congregation. It can begin when they drive past the church building and like what they see. It can begin when they read about the congregation, listen to discussions about it, and are interested in what they hear. Many people, though not as many as formerly, are first attracted to a congregation by its denominational label. Most people begin to form their impressions and expectations of a church before they participate in any activities. Usually these impressions are positive, or they wouldn't bother to visit! It is the congregation's responsibility to build on these hopeful attitudes.

A recent Gallup Poll tells us that 75 percent of us consider ourselves shy, inarticulate, uncomfortable around strangers, and hesitant to place ourselves in new situations. For 75 percent of us, attending a congregation's worship service for the first few times can be difficult, even terrifying experiences. Every congregation will want to take this situation seriously. The very least we can do is to welcome our newcomers warmly and make followup calls to get to know them better. It is the congregation's responsibility to show the newcomers that the congregation can help them strengthen their relationship with God and that they can find friends in the congregation who will support them and challenge them to grow.

It is not the purpose of this booklet to explore specific ways of attracting newcomers and of helping them make the decision to join the church formally. Such information is available. However, to talk about nurturing people, helping them mature as Christians once they have become members of the congregation, all the while ignoring what has happened in their lives as they were arriving at the decision to join, is much like ignoring all the growth and development that takes place in the life of the baby the nine months or so before the baby's birth.

Some babies benefit from a loving, careful prenatal environment; other babies are born with handicaps or deficiencies because of a careless or destructive prenatal environment. So, too, some new church members have grown stronger in faith and fellowship as they were deciding to become formal members of the congregation. They may be quite easy to

9

incorporate into the life and ministry of the congregation since the process has already begun successfully. This, of course, is the ideal situation and the one all of us strive for in our congregations; but it does not happen without a great deal of planning and effort. In fact, many of our new members have been wounded by their reception from the membership, or they haven't yet found the spiritual nourishment they seek. When they decide to join the congregation despite negative experiences, they may be "at risk" as they approach that ever-present crossroad of deeper participation versus increased inactivity.

One of the biggest mistakes we make is to assume that once newcomers have become members, everything is fine with them and that they don't need our careful attention any more. Every congregation needs people who sense the call to be close to new members as they move into a fuller relationship with the congregation. All of us who are concerned about closing those back doors in our congregations, through which hurt or neglected members flow, should work closely with those in our congregation who reach out to attract new members and with those who are committed to helping new members get well planted in the congregation's life and ministry. People drop out of active participation in church life for a wide variety of reasons, but most people drop out because they never got firmly settled in a congregation. Either their spiritual needs were not met, or they didn't find the deep friendship they wanted, or they weren't equipped to identify and use their gifts in God's service.

Some church sociologists estimate that between one-third and one-half of all members of Protestant churches in the United States are not comfortable with their church affiliation. Many do not feel that they have been welcomed into the fellowship except on a very superficial level. They feel marginal in the life of the congregation and they stand on the edge of inactivity.

To be sure, church members can be neglected during any stage of membership and can elect to leave the church at any time. This book concentrates on the new member and on that particularly vulnerable first year of membership, but many of the strategies suggested for helping new members find their place within the congregation can be—should be—part of a congregation's overall membership care plan.

New church members share a number of common experiences and hopes; however, the ways in which these hopes can be met depend, to some degree, on the size of the congregation, since the dynamics involved in attracting and incorporating new members vary somewhat in congregations of different sizes. Categories are seldom discreet, however;

therefore readers will do well to read the descriptions for all categories; then choose the suggestions that fit their congregations.

Congregations Averaging Approximately 50 at Worship

Congregations of this size are sometimes called single-cell churches, which describes how the congregation functions. In single-cell churches everyone knows everyone else and everyone takes an active interest in the lives of the other members. Someone has joked that in a single-cell church all the members would know not only that the Hatchers' son Mark is away at the state college, they would also know about his grades and the name of the girl he dates.

Carl Dudley, a keen observer of congregations this size, calls them "intimate communities." They are communities of people who depend on each other, a network in which everyone has a place. The community feels incomplete and uneasy whenever someone is absent without explanation because the network's pattern is then disturbed. These congregations are seldom interested in "issues" or societal "problems," but they are intensely concerned about their own hurting people. And when their people are hurting, they organize to get something done. Carl Dudley says that anyone can be "one of ours" if the connection between the person and the congregation can be made clear: e.g., a picture of a suffering South African plus a notation that the sufferer is a United Methodist also.

An intimate community is always larger than the number in attendance because it extends to those about whom the members care. When any of these hurt, the whole body hurts. In fact, much time is spent finding out how everyone is, having a "body check" so that individual members can know how they themselves are doing.

A small membership church that wants to grow would do well to look at these extended relationships (Who comes to weddings, funerals? Who brings food and comfort when members are sick?). These people are already part of the family and probably are kindred spirits as well. Some of them may attend church functions already. Some who may never be willing to join the institution would be happy to support the congregation with their prayers, presence, gifts, and service, if only asked. Indeed, congregations serious about helping their people grow as disciples will not be forgetful of their extended family.

A single-cell church or "intimate community" functions like a large family and is almost always controlled by a strong parental figure or two, commonly referred to as the church matriarch or patriarch—the head of the family. The matriarch or patriarch may or may not hold an official office in the church structure, but no decision is made without the approval of this figure. Actually most church decisions are made in informal settings and only ratified in scheduled meetings.

Again Carl Dudley reminds us that the leaders of these congregations are not leaders because of their training, skill, or office. They are the leaders because the other members trust them and are convinced that the leaders know and care about them. It is felt that like literal parents, the leaders know what's good for members, and they know what's going on with members even without being told, because they hurt when others in the congregation are hurting.

For many people, even the unchurched, a church building symbolizes God's presence and is, in some sense, a sacred place. This is especially true and evident in smaller membership churches. So much of the lives of members is related to the building and to the congregation's history that the building, grounds, and many objects in the church take on holy significance. Births, marriages, funerals, baptisms, countless acts of confession and commitment are relived as members interact. People sit where they do in order to be near people, some of whom are no longer alive. The atmosphere is rich with memories. Places and history are extraordinarily important in the life of the congregation.

The pastor of a congregation this size is hardly ever the head of the congregation. Usually the pastor serves more than the one congregation, is a student or other short-termer, and cannot be with the congregation enough to earn the role "head of the household." The pastor can play a very influential role in the congregation's life, however, by serving as chaplain or spiritual guide for the members. The pastor should also function as a gentle commentator on congregational life with comments such as, "I see . . . and . . . happening in our congregation. Is this what we want to continue to happen?" The gentle approach will be expedient as the pastor realizes there is an increased amount of bickering in this size congregation. Remember, brothers and sisters who are quite pleasant in public may spend all their time at home fighting with each other. Home is the place where they know they are free to fight, that they will not be thrown out for expressing their feelings. The same may be true in small membership congregations, since only close, intimate communities can risk conflict.

If the pastor is able to win the respect of the matriarch or patriarch, he/

she can work with these leaders to discern God's will for the congregation and can encourage and support the leaders as they guide the congregation.

New members usually join the small church because: (1) they have married a member or have close ties with some member; or (2) they have a strong denominational loyalty; or (3) the congregation is an important community institution, and the new member is highly committed to the community; or (4) the congregation is engaged in some distinctive ministry or service in which the newcomer wants to be involved. However, no matter what attracts new members, they cannot make a place for themselves: They must be *adopted* by the "family" in spirit, as well as in name, if they are to feel that they really do "belong." Only the laity of the church have the power to decide that the new member is now truly one of us and to make a place for the newcomer in the life and work of the congregation.

Incorporation in this church requires a great deal of intentional effort, and usually it doesn't happen quickly. Some people have been members of churches this size for years and years and still wonder if they are really part of the family. Anyone who has married and who has struggled to feel a part of his or her spouse's family can understand this new member's situation and feelings.

NEWCOMERS' NEEDS

In congregations this size, newcomers' needs, in addition to their spiritual concerns, include:

- *Knowledge, heritage, and traditions* of the congregation. A congregation this size often is more concerned than most with its past. The newcomers are likely to feel lost in many discussions until they begin to know some of the "family" history, legends, and important figures. Over the years, these stories can be picked up, just as the children in our biological families learn our family stories by hearing them repeatedly, by looking through picture albums, by spending time with grandparents, aunts, uncles, and other family members. However, adult new members of small membership churches seldom have the patience to wait the years and years it takes to learn informally the church's history. They need some immediate and specific help in this area. Furthermore, new members want to connect their own histories with the story of the congregation, to make the congregation's history their own and to have the congregation's history rewoven to include them. Native American peoples have a "sacred bundle" which contains objects, symbols of significance. Whenever a person is initiated into the tribe, the bundle is untied, and the sacred objects are examined and explained. Then the newcomer adds an object and the bundle is retied. Histories are interwoven.

Congregations can be sure newcomers know the congregation and are known themselves. Congregations can give newcomers opportunities to tell the congregation's stories and to find a place for themselves in the stories.

• A *mentor.* New members also need someone from whom they can learn more about other church members: Who is related to whom? Why does Mr. Murray seem to care so much about the altar flowers? Why do "Aunt" May and Mrs. Cory try to ignore each other? and so on. The relationships in churches this size are deep, often complicated, and usually confusing to newcomers. If they have someone with whom they can "safely" share their questions, and observations, they will understand the congregation more quickly. Often the pastor can serve as this person for the new member and also can help them work through their feelings about their new "brothers, sisters, uncles, and cousins."

• *Contact with the leadership.* Since the natural leaders of the congregation, the matriarch and/or patriarch, can cast the determining "vote" in whether or not to "adopt" new members into the family, it is very helpful if the newcomers are able to have gradual, intentional contact with these influential members. Often these contacts have to be engineered by someone who is trusted by the matriarch/patriarch and also is committed to helping new members find a place of belonging. These relationships will take time to develop. Trust must develop. Since the matriarch or patriarch embodies the congregation, newcomers won't be part of the congregation until they are known by the matriarch or patriarch. When heads of the congregation feel free to tell the newcomer their stories, and when they know that the newcomers have heard and share their pains and joys, then they will be ready to adopt them into the family.

• *Outside fellowship.* Since these congregations are sometimes comprised of just a few family groupings, and since deep relationships that involve all aspects of the members' lives are always important, new members need to have contact with other members in settings beyond the church. When the church is the focal point of the members' social lives, these contacts may develop naturally. But if the church is in an urban area, if members do not live in one area, or if the new member was initially attracted by some ministry of the congregation, an intentional effort may be needed to orchestrate opportunities for the new member to spend time with other members other than at worship or Sunday school.

• *Use gifts and talents.* In healthy families, all members feel that they are important and that they can contribute to the family's welfare. This is true in church families, too. In addition, in church life, people are concerned about discovering their God-given talents and about using these gifts to serve God, their neighbors, the church. When a new member has a gift the church has been needing, and when the new member will not replace a long-time member who is not yet ready to step aside, there is no problem. Unfortunately, situations usually are not so simple. Especially in congregations with fewer members, jobs tend to belong to specific people. No one can imagine anyone else doing them. All of this can be very frustrating to new members who feel frozen out of opportunities to serve and who, then, soon feel unneeded and unwanted by the congregation. The pastor or a sensitive, trusted layperson has to be attuned to: (a) the new-comer's gifts and callings, (b) to opportunities within the church and in the community where these gifts can be used, and also (c) to the feelings of longer term members.

PASTOR'S ROLE

The *pastor* of the congregation does not have the power to admit the newcomer into the family, but the pastor can:

• *Be a friend,* by specifically offering himself or herself as a spiritual guide and confidential friend. The pastor can say clearly and appropriately, "When you run into difficulty or uneasiness as you move into our church family, please let's talk about it. I'll be confidential and I'll support you as we work through the situation."

- *Identify mentors,* by noting which members are likely to help new members move into the fellowship circle of the church and by enlisting those people to be "special friends" of new members.

- *Observe the leadership,* by watching to see what usually happens that tells new members, "You are one of us." Is it when the new member is asked to be an usher? To help the women in the kitchen? Teach the adult Sunday school class? Help mow the lawn? Serve as a trustee? Most congregations have ways of showing people they really belong. Since this sort of behavior is largely subconscious, it takes someone like the pastor, who is also an outsider to a degree, to be able to see the dynamics. A trusted pastor can help some of the members see some of their unarticulated customs and can encourage them to include newcomers in some of the formerly closed activities.

- *Identify the "storytellers"* of the congregation—those people who know the history of the congregation and who are interested in telling the congregation's "stories." As the pastor visits the members, it will be easy to identify these people. The pastor who will engineer meetings between a storyteller and the new member will do both a great favor.

- *Educate the family and/or close friends of the new member* so they are aware of the ways congregations of this size receive and relate to new people. These people may have been part of the congregation their entire lives. It may never occur to them that the newcomer doesn't automatically feel accepted or comfortable. The pastor, or alert lay person, can ask these relatives or friends explicitly to help the new member get acquainted and learn about the life and ministry of the congregation.

As said before, it is the laity who have the power to include or exclude, to tolerate or to adopt. In a church this size, organizational structures are less important, while relationships are everything. It would be counterproductive to formally organize an incorporation committee, but it is important that an intentional effort be made to ease the new member's way into the congregation. The pastor may be able to see what needs to be done, but, by and large, the work will have to be done by the lay people who are trusted by the other members of the congregation.

Churches with 50 or less at worship	√	Our congregation . . .
General characteristics • Single-cell, intimate community, a complex network of relationships. • People-oriented, not issue-oriented. • Includes an extended family to which could minister more directly. • Church is a sacred place, filled with sacred objects and history. • Leaders take care of the family. • Pastors can be spiritual guides or loving commentators on church life. • Network of relationships is jarred by newcomers.		
Incorporates by • Adoption, being given a place in the family, in the network.		We incorporate by . . .
Possible strategies • Identify storytellers, link to newcomers. • Annual events at which history relived. • Mentors for newcomers. • Identify rituals that say, "You belong." • Explain sacred objects. • Identify gifts and callings of newcomers; use them.		

Congregations Averaging 50-175 at Worship

This size range includes widely varying congregations. Congregations that fall on either end of the spectrum may want to look at the descriptions given for churches in the next closest category. Read about the smaller membership church because much of that description also applies to this size range. Several additional observations also can be made.

Most congregations in this category have two or three cells. Each cell functions somewhat like the single-cell church, and the congregation still experiences strong family-like ties. But the church is now more like a large extended family. There are usually several matriarchs and patriarchs, and congregational life needs an organizer and some structure. The pastor moves to the center of the leadership circle, but since relationships are still the key ingredient in congregational life, leadership remains pastoral and relational. Because everyone expects a lot of attention from the pastor, and because all the members want to stay in touch with each other, there are a lot of existing relationships to manage. There isn't much energy left over for newcomers. This size congregation frequently congratulates itself on being a "friendly church." Visitors often comment that the members may be friendly to each other, but they certainly aren't friendly to the stranger. The fact is that most members don't even see visitors because they are so busy trying to see and to keep up with each other. The church's history continues to be important, and the building(s) and furnishings are sacred objects for many members. Newcomers may not need to know all the stories but they, like newcomers in single-cell churches, do need to be sensitive to these issues.

It sometimes happens that members of churches on the upper side of this size-range have subconsciously decided they don't want their church to get any bigger. There are already more people than they can know well, and it is important to them to know all the other members. With this attitude, growth and successful incorporation of new members is very difficult.

On the other hand, the two- or three-cell church that does want to grow has several strong advantages: Personal, family-like ties are valued and encouraged; members can expect a lot of attention from the pastor; and there is more programming and small group life than in the one-cell church. These congregations do not revolve around their programs, but they usually do have more than one or two entry points into their fellowship circle.

NEWCOMERS' NEEDS

Newcomers are attracted by the strong relational nature of the congregation. Most people hope to deepen their relationship with God when they become part of God's church. People who are attracted to churches of this size tend to feel that they are most likely to find God's presence and love in their relationships with others. They, too, will expect a lot of attention from the pastor; indeed, the pastor is most likely to be the person who brings them into the life and ministry of the church. Some new members may marry into the congregation, some may first visit the congregation because it is a neighborhood institution, or because of denominational loyalty. Most will stay only if they are able to experience some of the relational closeness valued by congregations of this size.

In addition to their spiritual needs, newcomers need:

- *Careful nurturing* by the pastor coupled with purposeful attention by several people. New members do not need to know everyone as they would in the single-cell church, but they do need to know quickly, and be known by eight to ten people. Loving attention by a few lay people tells the new members that the congregation's claim to be a caring fellowship is not an empty one, and that there may indeed be places for them within the fellowship.

- *History.* New members will also want to know some of the history of the congregation. While this will not be quite so crucial as in the single-cell church, it is quite important for the new member to know why the congregation does what it does and what the congregation views as its current mission. New members also want to understand what the congregation expects from them.

- *Ports of entry.* Newcomers will need help in discovering the groups and/or service opportunities that best fit them and their gifts. Groups in congregations in this size range may function much like the single-cell congregation, but since there are multiple cells, newcomers have more opportunities to find one that suits them. And unless the congregation has decided not to grow any more, it may be receptive to beginning a new group in an effort to meet the needs of the new members.

Churches with 50-175 at worship	√	Our congregation . . .
General characteristics • Several cells, several interrelated networks, several points of entry. • Relationships still paramount. • Pastor, a focal point, expected to know all members. • Good communication important. • May not want to grow bigger. • Some programming, maybe. • Willing to begin new groups.		
Incorporates by • Recognize, welcome newcomers. • Developing relationships with pastor and several lay people. • Sharing history. • Placing in a group or network. • Identifying and using gifts.		
Possible strategies • Develop system for greeting, welcoming, following up on newcomers. • Spiritual formation visits, groups. • Connect members with gift of hospitality to newcomers. • New member classes. • Orientation programs. • Plant newcomer in a group. • Identify and use gifts of newcomer. • Careful recordkeeping. • Fellowship events.		We incorporate by . . .

PASTOR'S TASK

The task of the pastor in the process of incorporating new members into the life of the congregation must be considered carefully. Congregations this size tend to see evangelism and visitation with newcomers as the pastor's job. After all, the lay people have their hands full keeping up with all the friends they already have in the congregation. The pastor may be agreeable to this situation and even may find that it is the newcomers who are most receptive to the pastor's dreams for the congregation.

The pastor does know the congregation well and is able to guide the newcomers as they try to find their places. This responsibility takes a great deal of time. Most pastors can recruit and manage the incorporation process for only six to ten people a year. Furthermore, when the pastor, who has been giving a fairly recent new member a lot of attention, must switch some energy and attention to potential members or to other new members, the former recipient of the attention may feel rejected and lonely. Unless the pastor has recruited and trained several people to accept some of the responsibility for developing relationships with new members, the number of people who can be incorporated per year into the life of the church will be small, and there may be a number of members whose loyalty is to the pastor rather than to the congregation.

Those who discover that they have a gift of hospitality and are willing to help newcomers move into the fellowship circle should not become an administrative group. The responsibility for and power of admitting new members into the fellowship still lie with the whole congregation. Those who agree to assist the pastor should be chosen for their relational skills and commitment to helping newcomers develop supportive relationships within the congregation.

In short, the role to be played by the *laity* in congregations in this size-range include: (1) being intentional about recognizing newcomers, about welcoming them, and about helping them become part of depth relationships; (2) being aware of which groups are likely to be open and welcoming to newcomers and to help establish new groups if they are needed; (3) provide an orientation for new members to both the history of the congregation and the current goals of the congregation.

Congregations Averaging More Than 175 at Worship

Many congregational types have been lumped together under this category. A church averaging two hundred at worship obviously is quite different from the church with eight hundred at worship, which is different in many ways from the congregation that has several thousand at worship. However, once a congregation reaches a certain level of structural complexity, there are some common trends in the ways new members move into the life and ministry of the church.

The life of large membership congregations tends to revolve around worship and programs. Worship may be inspirational, even awesome, with outstanding choirs, liturgies, and preaching. Programs frequently are extremely well conceived and executed, which strengthens the belonging of the participants in such programs. Newcomers are attracted by the quality of the programs and worship service. A lot of people enjoy being part of something that feels significant even if for no other reason than that so many other people seem to find it meaningful.

Personal relationships and friendships are much harder to develop in large churches and may have some characteristics that differ from friendships formed in churches with fewer members. Relationships usually form as people participate in small groups. Some of these groups will be long-term ongoing groupings such as Sunday school classes or women's circles or choirs. Other groups will be more short-term and spontaneous and may even spring up almost overnight to address a current issue, meet some need, or field a church athletic team. There are likely to be some study courses which have definite timelines, and there are always layers of organizational groups which manage the business of the congregation. In all of these settings people may develop significant relationships. In large membership churches there can be quite a large number of functioning groups. Unfortunately, the new member may not know about the groups or may not know how to go about becoming part of one of the groups.

Even when new members do participate in some of the groups, they often find it hard to develop friendships that become significant and relevant outside the walls of the church. Members of large membership churches tend to treat the congregation like a spiritual supermarket from which they can obtain a little of this, a little of that, as the need arises. Furthermore, since it is obvious that there are so many people available to do the administrative work of the congregation and to be involved in its outreach ministry, it is quite easy for people to assume they aren't needed. And again, since congregational life is so complex, it can be perplexing to understand its inner workings. The result too frequently is that church activities may be handled in very functional ways: "Let's do what we came to do and get out of here." This attitude, so prevalent in our over-scheduled world, makes developing and nurturing significant friendships very difficult, and people who do not develop significant friendships within their church associations are at risk of becoming inactive members.

It is easy to be lost in a large membership church. It is easy to hide in a large membership church, to feel no obligation to participate in any activity other than worship. In fact, some people join large membership churches because they hope to be anonymous and to be lost in the crowds. Often these folks have worked themselves to burnout in other congregations, and they want a rest. Others are shy and hesitant to push themselves into visibility. All churches do well to learn as much as possible about their newcomers and to honor their needs. This does not mean that churches should ignore those who want to rest or who are slow to participate in activities other than worship. Regular, intentional contacts can be made so that the congregation can know when the person is ready to move more deeply into congregational life. Those who are lost and those who are hiding are likely to find that back door leading to inactivity if they are left totally unattended. Many vital large membership churches keep very careful records of the participation level of all their members so that they can respond when attendance and participation patterns begin to change.

Many churches this size find that it is not hard to attract new members, but it can be very hard to incorporate them into the life and ministry of the congregation.

NEWCOMERS' NEEDS

Newcomers to large membership churches need very intentional and specific assistance in moving into active participation and are helped particularly by:

- *A packet of information* on the congregation, including the congregation's mission statement with a description of current and planned ministries; a diagram of the church building; a listing of ongoing groups (for all ages) and their meeting sites; a description of current and planned programs; pictures of the staff and membership of the congregation.

- An ongoing *organized program* of incorporating new members which welcome, gather visitor information, follow up with visitation, provide opportunities for orientation to the congregation and denomination, help newcomers find small groups, identify their gifts and match their gifts with opportunities for ministry.
- A *new member sponsor program* which ensures that new members are befriended by a lay person who is committed to helping the newcomer find a comfortable, yet challenging, place in the congregation and who will be careful to introduce the newcomer to other people in the congregation with whom friendships might develop.
- An ongoing system of *monitoring* the participation pattern of new members which lets the new members know that they are missed when absent and that the congregation is concerned when they encounter difficulties. In large membership churches it is very easy not to notice that a person is participating less and less until that person is "gone for good." A system of monitoring attendance and of responding to changing patterns of attendance is one way to say "we care."
- A *clear statement* of how the congregation expects to help the newcomer grow in ability and willingness to receive God's love and to respond to God's love in service to others. Such a statement would also state as clearly as possible the church's expectations of the new member.

The *laity* of the large membership church are the ones who must manage the process of incorporating new members. In most churches a special task force will be required and a specific step-by-step program will be developed and administered. The *clergy* of the church, of course, will want to be involved—perhaps in teaching new member classes, hosting new member luncheons or dinners, writing letters of welcome, etc. New members seldom expect personal friendship with the senior minister, but they will want to think that such a relationship is possible and especially that the senior pastor and staff will be with them in times of trouble or stress. People do not join churches if they do not like or admire the staff, but in the large membership church it is the laity who will provide the significant welcome and nurture.

Churches, more than 175 at worship	√	Our congregation . . .
General characteristics • Worship and programs at the center of congregational life. • High quality worship, programs. • Complex organizational and administrative structures. • Good communication essential. • Dynamic group life. • Easy for newcomers to get lost or to be forgotten.		
Incorporates by • Having an intentional process that creates a path through the maze of congregational life and ministry. • Placing in a group. • Identifying and using gifts.		
Possible strategies • Task force to manage processes. • Develop and use a packet of information about the congregation. • Spiritual formation visits, groups. • New member classes. • Orientation opportunities. • New member sponsor program. • Small group participation. • Identify and use gifts. • Neighborhood/shepherding program. • Church-wide events.		We incorporate by . . .

3. NEW MEMBERS' NEEDS

We have considered briefly some of the dynamics encountered by newcomers to our churches. In this chapter we will look more closely at several of the needs that new members apparently have regardless of the size of the congregation which they join.

First of all, we believe that *people come to our churches looking for hope and for meaning in their lives.* To be sure, people turn to churches when they have physical, social, or emotional needs and when the present situation is cared for, they too have a longing to know that God loves them and has high hopes for them. People expect that the church can help them hear what God is saying to them. *People want the church to help them see how God is involved in their everyday lives.* People need the church to help them respond to God's activity in their lives and in the world. To repeat the obvious, people turn to the church for spiritual and religious reasons.

Often people turn to the church following some change in their lives— a weathering of a crisis, a piece of extremely good luck, some change in the pattern of their lives. When the routine of their lives is upset, before new patterns are established, people are able to think about God and about God's promises and claims in new ways. Often they want the church to guide and support them during this transition. They expect the church to be serious about helping them live out the Christian journey and life.

For new members and long-term members as well, it is essential that the congregation have a core of Christian integrity and seriousness. Likewise, it is crucial that congregations be committed fully to encouraging members' growth as disciples of Jesus the Christ.

This story illustrates how one congregation in the northeastern United States has begun to help its members be serious about their relationship with God and about God's relationship with the world:

> A young pastor recently appointed to a new church opened his first Administrative Council meeting with the question: "Where have you seen God at work lately—or heard of God being at work?" The handful of people who had bothered to show up at the meeting were

clearly uncomfortable with the question: they squirmed in their seats and refused to meet the pastor's wondering gaze. The pastor allowed the question to hang in the air for an unpleasant length of time, then quietly moved on to other matters. The pastor did not rush to remedy an awkward situation with a quick platitude.

At the next Administrative Council meeting, again sparsely attended, the pastor began with the question, "Well, where have you seen God at work since we last met?" Once more the room was filled with discomfort and squirming avoidance. Once more the pastor allowed the question to work on those present and did not rush in with easy responses.

The third meeting—"Where have you seen God at work since we last met?" Finally after another long distressed silence, one woman reached into her handbag, pulled out a newspaper clipping and said, "I don't know if this is what you mean, but . . . " The discussion was off and running. And it wasn't only the discussion that was loosened up. The pastor reports that in the months following that breakthrough meeting, attendance at the Administrative Council has quadrupled, and worship attendance has doubled. The pastor says, "I can only attribute this to asking that question!"

What a difference it makes when a congregation's members become convinced that the church is serious about helping them relate to God and about helping them have opportunities to discuss with others, face-to-face, what God has done and what God might be calling them to do in response.

It has been said repeatedly that well-fed sheep cannot be stolen, and it is surely true that people who feel that they are growing spiritually are unlikely to stray from the church into inactivity.

The congregation that would be serious about helping new members explore ways of living out the Christian life and journey, will want to consider including several of the following strategies in their incorporation process. Each of the strategies will be discussed at more length in Chapter 4. They are mentioned here as illustrations of the sorts of activities that help newcomers understand that the congregation is committed to fostering their growth in discipleship.

- *Spiritual guidance visits* in the homes of new or prospective members to give them a chance to explore quietly where they are in their relationship with God and neighbor

- *A membership class* series which clarifies the Christian story, the newcomer's story, and then calls for decisions about what commitments the newcomer is ready to make

- A meaningful *service of reception* into the membership of the congregation

- *Serious study* that results in fresh commitment

- Opportunities for *identifying* one's *gifts* and *talents* and assistance in finding ways to use identified gifts

- Programs, sermons, studies that facilitate an understanding of the spiritual dimensions of participating in intentional stewardship of money and of others of God's resources

A second need that newcomers bring with them as they begin the process of being incorporated is the need to know and to be known by other members, to feel accepted into the life and ministry of the congregation. Some pastors do report that they have people joining their churches who say they want only a place to worship. They declare clearly by their word or their actions that they are interested in no deeper or broader relationship with the congregation. This understanding of worship as a solitary endeavor is curious, and we believe, antithetical to true worship. We believe that no matter what one's attitude upon joining, one will eventually be moved to desire a deeper level of participation and fellowship, or one will fall away from the congregation altogether. It is the congregation's responsibility to stay close enough to the fringe members that their changed attitude will be noticed and acted upon.

Again much has been written about how marginal members find ways into the fellowship circles; yet, almost all observers agree that two things must happen for most people if they are to develop a sense of belonging: (1) They must develop several meaningful friendships which draw them into the larger fellowship, and (2) they must be able to contribute some of their own effort, skill, and energy to the life and ministry of the congregation. People begin to develop a sense of belonging when they know they are missed, if absent, and when they know they are needed to enhance the functioning of the Body.

In smaller membership churches small groups are not an issue, but in larger congregations, when considering how a congregation can help new members feel accepted and important to the congregation, it would be difficult to overstate the significance of helping newcomers become part of small groups and of helping them to find jobs or roles that utilize their gifts. Some strategies which the laity of the incorporation committee may want to consider are:

- *Evaluate existing small groups* as to their openness to newcomers and enlist the aggressive support of those groups still open. Consider possibilities for new small groups, and begin a reasonable number. (See pages 59-61 for guidelines.)

- Allow new members to assume *leadership roles* or tasks appropriate to their gifts and sense of calling. (See pages 54-58 for guidelines.)

- Institute a program of *systematic visitation* of prospective and new members with the purpose of getting to know these people.

- *Establish a sponsor/shepherd program* dedicated to making newcomers known to the congregation. (See pages 66-68 for guidelines.)

- *Create fellowship:* neighborhood get-togethers, potluck dinners before educational programs, camping trips, sightseeing trips, work projects around the church property, work projects in the community, hobby classes, and so on. These activities should not undercut the efforts of existing small groups to develop fellowship; they merely give people chances to socialize across group lines and to broaden their friendship base within the congregation.

- Monitor the *attendance patterns* and participation patterns of all members, especially among newcomers. A call after three consecutive absences that says, "We've been missing you, is everything all right?" helps people know they are important to the group and to the congregation. (See pages 39-45 for guidelines.)

The third area of widespread concern to newcomers is their need to know about the congregation's history as well as current ministry goals in order to be able to discover where their gifts and calling might best fit in.

People join churches because they hope that the current commitments and goals of the congregation will match their own needs and their own concerns for God's world. Newcomers are not automatically interested in the history and long-past achievements of the congregations. In contrast, long-time members tend much more to face the past when they think about the congregation. The building has become a sacred place for them. Past triumphs of the congregation still fill them with a sense of accomplishment and past disappointments may still live with them. Past relationships still nurture them. For example, almost every church has some spot that is left vacant in the sanctuary because that was beloved Aunt Mary's place. Long-time members often feel surrounded by a "cloud of witnesses" that is invisible to newcomers and which many long-time members fear may be dispelled by unrespectful newcomers.

"Stranger means danger" is an axiom that people have believed and acted upon apparently forever. We who wish to help newcomers move into a meaningful relationship with our congregations will want to find ways to help them seem less like strangers to our long-time members.

Several years ago, Suzanne and Jack were married. Every Christmas day they joined his family at his grandmother's house for a festive Christmas dinner. On her first Christmas with her new family, Suzanne was interested in all the excitement caused by the arrival at the table of the cranberry sauce. Someone explained to her that the cranberry sauce bowl had a great significance to "greatmomma"— her new grandmother-in-law.

The next year, Suzanne had to be reminded why the cranberry sauce caused such a stir around the Christmas dinner table. By the third Christmas, although she had forgotten again the significance of the bowl, she remembered to "ooh and aah" with everyone else when the cranberries were brought to the table.

Within a few years, hosting Christmas dinner was too large a task for "greatmomma," so the celebration moved to Suzanne's and Jack's house. Each year greatmomma arrived with the cranberry sauce; each year everyone "ooh'd and aah'd." Suzanne joined in, the time long past when she could again ask why the bowl was important. Really it was enough just to recognize the importance of the bowl to make her very nervous until the bowl, carefully washed and dried, was back safely in greatmomma's hands.

One year as greatmomma was leaving, she was handed her bowl. She stopped, handed the bowl back to Suzanne and said, "I want you to keep the bowl!"

Every time Suzanne opens her cabinet and sees the "Christmas cranberry bowl" she is touched, and she knows that she is truly a part of her husband's family. But she still doesn't remember why the bowl is important to the others!

Every congregation has sacred "cranberry bowls." It isn't necessary that new members remember why these sacred objects (or events) are important, but it is necessary that new members recognize the importance of such events and honor them for the sake of those other members. Long-time members don't fear new things or new ways of doing things as much as they fear that those things important to them will be done away with. If we can assure them that their needs will not be violated, they will be much more relaxed about letting newer members try some things their way. New members need help if they are to avoid violating some sacred place or object or event. One way to provide this help is to provide opportunities for newcomers to hear and to honor the stories and faith commitments of the longer-term members.

In addition, new members will welcome opportunities to explore their own gifts and callings. New members are interested in the present and the future of the congregation and want to discover how they can become a functioning part of this Body of Christ. Some strategies to consider, which help newcomers honor the heritage of the congregation:

- "Homecoming" events when newcomers can celebrate stories from the past as well as share dreams for the future.

- Storytelling events which develop friendships with long-term members: adopt-a-grandparent program, tours of church property given by "storytellers," celebrate our heritage days in Sunday school classes, etc.

- *Membership classes* which teach the history as well as the contemporary situation and commitments of the congregation and the denomination. (See pages 46-51 for guidelines.)

- Gift and talent classes which establish a strong system for helping people discover, claim, and use their gifts and their sense of God's calling.

Questions for consideration: Make a list of the last (10) (5) (3) people who have joined your church and/or consider several of your prospective members and put down their names.

Names	Their needs/hopes	Congregation's current pertinent ministries	Ministries we might consider

Part Two

SEVEN PROVEN STRATEGIES

Does your congregation have an incorporation problem? Evaluate your situation by discussing the following questions, and use the following survey with your new members.

Questions for an Incorporation Committee

1. Make a list of the last 10 (5), (3) people who have joined your congregation. What are their current levels of participation?

   - How often are they in worship?
   - In what small groups are they involved?
   - In what ways have they been challenged to use their gifts/skills/ money in the congregation and/or in the community?
   - Have they had an opportunity to talk about their relationship with the congregation? (See questionnaire below.)

2. In the last three years, how many people who have not changed their residency have transferred their membership from your congregation?
3. What is the difference between your number of members and the number of people in worship each Sunday?
4. What percentage of your membership is at worship only once a month or less?
5. What is the difference between your Sunday school enrollment figure and your average Sunday school attendance?
6. Are there members whose level of involvement has declined in the last two months?

These questions suggest that the areas in which your congregation could improve its ministry to and with newcomers are:

1.

2.

3.

What seems to be working well that you can build on?

NEW MEMBER SURVEY

A congregation could request new members to complete and return a survey such as this. However, better information will be gathered if the congregation will train people to ask these questions of new members *and* to listen to their responses without defensiveness.

1. The things that attracted me most to this congregation were:
2. When I first attended I felt:
3. The thing that most encouraged me to join was:
4. The new member training/orientation was:
5. I currently am participating in:
6. I might like to participate in:
7. One of the concerns I have about our congregation is:
8. One of the concerns I have about our community is:
9. This congregation is helping me grow spiritually by:
10. In general, I feel:
    —Extremely good about being a member of this congregation.
    —Basically satisfied with my reception and participation level.
    —Somewhat disappointed with the congregation.
    —About to look for another church.

GETTING STARTED

1. Read through the first three chapters of this book.
2. Have one or more of the task force report their evaluation of your congregation using the appropriate chart in Chapter Two. Discuss.
3. Have one or more of the task force fill in the chart at the end of Chapter Three and report their assessment and recommendations. Discuss.
4. Evaluate your response to the questions for an Incorporation Committee and the responses made to the New Member Survey.
5. List recommendations to be made to your Administrative Council or Board.
6. Develop new strategies or strengthen old ones using a combination of the seven specific approaches that follow.

Celebrate the richness and vitality of a congregation walking the pathways of growth!

STRATEGY I

Visitation Programs

Some experienced pastors, lay leaders, and observers of congregational life recommend that if a church is to be intentional about outreach and growth, an active, vibrant visitation program is essential. Furthermore, it is argued that people today are more open to visits from church members than they have been in some decades. One recent study surveyed the subjects of an aggressive confrontational visitation program. Only 6 percent of these people reported negative reactions to the visits they received!

This is not to suggest or recommend aggressive, confrontational visits. We believe that people have deeper, more meaningful experiences when relationships are nurtured so that trust and mutual concern become part of the foundation on which faith grows. Nevertheless, the study does tell us that people may be more receptive to discussions about faith than we have thought. At the very least, people have positive reactions to the interest shown in them.

When people take the first step toward the church by attending worship or other activities, or when they have expressed interest in becoming a part of the congregation, they are very likely to welcome a visit from a church representative. Although the pastor is a very important person to newcomers, a person with whom they hope to have a personal relationship, not all visits made to newcomers should be made by the pastor. On some level almost everyone wonders if the pastor or staff person is visiting because he/she is interested or because that person's job description says he/she must visit. A visit by a lay person offers the newcomer the opportunity to know some of the others sitting with them in the pews, and it says to them that the lay people are so excited about the congregation that they want to share their enthusiasm with others. This is a powerful realization to the newcomer.

A well-designed and executed visitation program provides the following opportunities:

- To learn more about the newcomers, their personal history, faith, hopes and hurts.

- To share what is happening in the church's life and ministry.
- To provide spiritual nurture and challenge for those being called upon and for the callers.
- To help newcomers know some members.

Effective visitation programs require a lot of management. Often we are tempted to just do the work ourselves. We should resist the temptation. To recruit, train, and encourage participants in ongoing visitation program is to help them grow spiritually, to grow in ability, to love God, and neighbor.

Visitation programs should be designed according to a congregation's style and the needs of those to whom the congregation is reaching out. Resources listed at the end of this section describe various models and styles. A congregation would be wise to look at several resources and then to design a system that fit its concerns.

Several areas do need consideration in any program:

RECRUITMENT/VISITORS

1. Recruit, in person, people who have a genuine concern for others and a love for the church, as well as ability and willingness to talk about faith concerns. Help people determine whether or not they are called to this ministry.
2. Have visitors make a commitment to visit at specific times; for example, every Tuesday or every fourth Sunday, etc. Release them from any other church responsibilities that hamper their energy for this work. Nothing they do will be more important to their neighbors, themselves, or the congregation.

OTHERS NEEDED

Most congregations have several members who understand the need for a visitation program but who are unable (housebound, poor health, etc.) to make personal visits or who are uncomfortable doing so. These people are often eager to support the program by managing the card system and follow-up needs, by providing food or by praying for those involved in the program. Such people play an essential role in the success of any visitation program and should be recognized and thanked for their contributions.

TRAINING

An absolutely essential ingredient in an effective program is education. It need not be long or elaborate. People learn much more visiting than they do in a training session; but regular opportunities to increase skills and to clarify their own faith experiences encourages people and helps them grow spiritually. Many churches with effective visitation report that they provide short training periods for people almost every time they visit. All the resources listed at the end of this section include material to be used for training visitors. Topics to consider:

- Bible study—especially stories of the interactions between people
- Listening skills
- Faith-sharing skills
- Information on ways the church can support those they visit

Those people managing the information cards also need specific detailed instructions, although recurring training may not be necessary.

PASTORS/STAFF

The congregation's pastor and staff must demonstrate their commitment to this important ministry by being visible visitors themselves. Certainly, they should not do all the visiting, but they must not delegate all the visiting, no matter how well trained or dedicated the laity. Ken Callahan, in *Twelve Keys to an Effective Church* (Harper & Row), suggests that a pastor visit one hour per week for each minute of preaching!

Many congregations with effective visitation programs are organized for making at least two types of visits with newcomers: 1) a friendly, "We're glad you are here and we'd like to know you better" visit, and 2) an intentional faith-sharing and invitation or "spiritual formation" visit. *Visiting Two-by-Two* (Discipleship Resources) calls these types of visits "Good Neighbor" visits and "Good News" visits.

Some churches find that several friendly visits (Good Neighbor visit) which deepen friendships and trust are required before most people are truly receptive to an invitation to make new faith or church commitments (Good News visit, Spiritual Formation visit).

While the content and intensity of these two kinds of visits may differ, organizational structures can be shared. The following outline is recommended by many growing congregations.

Visitation Program Outline

- Lay volunteers or staff prepare cards with the names and addresses of those to be called upon. Pertinent information such as ages, children, interests, and friends in the congregation should be included. Appointments, if deemed necessary, should be made and noted on the cards.
- At designated time, pastor/staff meet lay visitors, preferably at the church.
- If appropriate, a simple snack meal is waiting.
- A brief (twenty minutes) training session is worked through—perhaps as people eat.
- Cards, prepared with names and pertinent information about those to be visited, are distributed. Two or three cards go to each team making first-time, friendly visits and probably only one card goes to teams making "spiritual formation" calls. It is best if the "spiritual formation" calls have been pre-arranged with the newcomer and a time agreed upon. Thoughts differ on whether or not to call ahead to schedule a friendly visit. Certainly, teams run the risk of finding no one home or the time inconvenient if they arrive without an appointment. But many people report that newcomers are reluctant to agree to a visit and will put them off repeatedly. Nine times out of ten the newcomer will be appreciative of an unannounced call and quite receptive—especially if the visitors are careful to keep the call short and friendly.
- A time of prayer, silent as well as audible, is shared. Every effort is made to avoid allowing this prayer time to become perfunctory or rushed.
- Teams leave to make their calls. Detailed guidelines for the visits are given in the resources listed at the end of this section. *Visiting Two-by-Two* and *Faith-Sharing* (both available from Discipleship Resources) are especially helpful.
- If travel time allows, teams return to the church to share their experiences and to make suggestions for possible follow-up with those visited. The visiting teams agree upon standards of confidentiality which must be strictly followed. This time for reporting can be vitally important to the whole program and should be required if at all possible. In fact, it would be better to ask each team to make one less call than to forego the report. If someone has come upon a puzzling situation or reaction, he/she can ask for suggestions about how to react in similar situations in the future. Even so, almost everyone will

have some positive experience to share that will encourage and spiritually energize the other visitors.
● Volunteers or staff update church records, noting the date of the call,
visitors who made the call, and any pertinent information learned.

Spiritual Formation Calls

Many people today are suggesting that one of the best ways of training
laity to make spiritual direction calls is to have two lay persons join the
pastor or an experienced lay person for these calls. The lay people are
prepared to take the lead in parts of the visit, but in general they watch
and learn as the pastor lovingly asks a version of John Wesley's question:
"How are things with you and God?" After several months, when the lay
people feel comfortable and confident with the question and responses,
they each take two new lay people with them to train as they were trained.

Rarely can a team make more than two of these calls in one evening or
afternoon. In fact, some teams report that their involvement level is so
high that only one visit per day is feasible. These calls should not surprise
the newcomer. They should be scheduled with the newcomers when there
is reason to think they will be receptive and for a time when they will be
able to give the call their undivided attention.

The purpose of these visits is to help people clarify their relationship
with God. The callers will be skillful listeners. They will be able to explore
with those they visit possible next steps for growth. They will not have
easy, pat suggestions or blunt judgments, but they will be able to share
what helped them grow or resources that have helped others. Equally
significant, they can report to the congregation spiritual needs or interests that can become the topics of sermons, Sunday school classes, or
study groups. Whenever, four or six people express an interest in an area,
there is an opportunity to begin a short-term study group. See pages
59-61 for guidelines for beginning new groups.

For individual study there are numerous available resources. People
making spiritual growth visits will want to be familiar with the Pass-
It-On-Books available from Discipleship Resources which present in
easy-to-understand language the major facets of the Christian faith and
experience. Also, they will want to note the broad range of topics and
situations addressed in tracts and leaflets also available from Discipleship
Resources. Some of these address a multitude of life situations; others,
United Methodist history and traditions; others, creeds and prayers of the

church; and still others encourage people to consider the ministries in their communities to which they are being called. All of these resources are written in concise, non-dogmatic language, and many people have found them very helpful.

These resources can be shared with people with the understanding that the visitors will return at an agreed-upon time for further discussion and mutual exploration.

Visiting Two-by-Two provides excellent practical guidelines for making spiritual guidance visits.

BEGIN A VISITATION PROGRAM

1. Review resources.
2. Recruit visitors.
3. Recruit people to support the program
   —to provide meals;
   —to prepare cards on those to be visited;
   —to post information gathered by the visitors;
   —to pray for those making calls and for those being called upon.
4. Write job descriptions.
5. Provide training, both initial and ongoing.
6. VISIT—VISIT—VISIT.
7. Keep the congregation informed, celebrate the growth, and thank those who participate.

Resources

Several excellent resources are available from Discipleship Resources, 1908 Grand Avenue, P. O. Box 189, Nashville, Tennessee 37202 (615-340-7284):

1. *Visiting Two-by-Two Filmstrip Packet* (no. V132P)
   A visitor's guide, filmstrip, and assorted leaflets for those preparing to represent their congregations as teams in calling on people in the community—a ministry through visiting. During a five-session training program, guidelines for making both "Good Neighbor" and "Good News" visits are given.

2. *A Ministry to Inactives* (no. EV143B)
   A manual for establishing a listening witness to inactive church members by Gerhard Knutson. Includes helps for listening and witnessing ministries and how to start a ministry to the inactives in your church. (*Augsburg*)

3. *Faith-Sharing: Dynamic Christian Witnessing by Invitation* (no. DR039B)
   A book which describes the content of the Christian faith, the setting of the evangelizing process, and the identity of the faith-sharer. Also includes principles and guidelines for sharing Jesus Christ with relatives, friends, and house-to-house. By H. Eddie Fox and George E. Morris.

STRATEGY II

Membership Classes

Membership classes traditionally are classes required or expected of new members. Often they are essentially orientation classes attended by people before or immediately after they join the church.

There is some controversy about the question of membership classes and their purposes. Some say that The United Methodist Church should be more specific about our distinctiveness and more demanding in our expectations of loyalty from our members. They mention John Wesley and his insistence that people belong to societies for nurture, accountability, and training. They feel that new members think that little is expected of them; therefore, new members invest little and soon drop out. They insist that new member classes are the place to teach people about the Christian faith in general and specifically about The United Methodist Church and a particular congregation. Once people have been through the course, they can decide whether or not they are ready to commit themselves to Christ and to the congregation.

Others argue that it is important to communicate obligations and congregational expectations, but this should not be the focus of the new member class. This position holds that the purpose of the new member class (which can be attended after joining) is to continue the incorporation process. The purpose of the new member class is to help people develop relationships with other members and find a meaningful service ministry in the congregation.

Still others insist that the new member class should do all of the above: ground people in the faith and practice of Christianity, a denomination, and a congregation—as well as challenge them to deeper personal, spiritual growth while they are making friends and finding their place of service within or through the congregation.

To be sure, new members usually have all of these needs, and each congregation has a process for meeting the needs. The process may not be an effective one; it may even be a version of "Let's see how long it takes them to guess what's going on around here." Your congregation should evaluate your current process for helping new members.

GOALS FOR A MEMBERSHIP CLASS

- Acknowledge the gospel story and challenge for commitment.
- Discover the distinctiveness of The United Methodist Church.
- Experience the sacraments and the worship style of the congregation.
- Decide what commitments new members are ready to make.
- Listen to the history and practices of your congregation.
- Meet and develop friendships with other members.
- Identify new members' gifts and find a place of service.
- Accept the promise and challenge of participating in the basic disciplines of the Christian life.

To accomplish all of the above in one series of membership classes would require months of meetings and, at least, six to eight class members. Many people are unwilling to commit themselves to twelve, sixteen, or twenty-four weeks of classes. Many churches do not have enough new members to start new member classes every few weeks, and the new member who must wait months for a class may grow impatient and drop out.

One solution to both problems is to offer as often as feasible a four- to six-week class designed as closely as possible to address the needs of those in the classes. Components that cannot be scheduled into the four- to six-week period, or which need further elaboration, can become the subject matter of another series of classes. Free catalog available from Discipleship Resources, P. O. Box 189, 1908 Grand Avenue, Nashville, Tennessee 37202.

For small membership churches, these classes might be individual or small group study sessions with the pastor at a time other than Sunday morning. Larger membership churches with a regular flow of new members would do well to consider the possibility that each new member class will become a new class or group within the life of the congregation. People who have spent four to six weeks together can be already far down the road of becoming significant in each other's lives and may want to continue to explore together the faith, a new place, and new relationships. Each group could then decide the order in which it would address the issues important to newcomers.

START A MEMBERSHIP CLASS

Set a congregational policy for new member classes. Questions to consider include:

1. Will they be required of all new members?
2. Will they fall before or after reception into membership?
3. When will the class meet? Where? For how long? What is the general purpose(s) of the class?
4. Will there be a standard course of study?
5. What study material will be made available?
6. Who will lead?
7. Will members for whom there were no such classes or who did not participate in confirmation classes be allowed (or expected) to attend?

Begin a Class

1. Make a prospect list of newest members, those considering joining, adults who haven't been through a confirmation class, etc.
2. Talk with the people on the prospect list. Analyze their needs, interests, concerns, and hopes. What components of a new member class will best suit their needs? List. What day and time is best for them? What else, such as child care, needs to be considered?
3. Secure leadership for the class. The leader should be someone with a firm understanding of the issues to be discussed. Many pastors like to lead or closely oversee the class because they are comfortable with the material and because this is a good opportunity to get to know newcomers.
5. Choose resources.
6. Begin!

Resources

Many excellent resources are available from Discipleship Resources, P. O. Box 189, 1908 Grand Avenue, Nashville, TN 37202 (615-340-7284). To explain the gospel story and challenge, see:
1. *A New Adventure in the Meaning of United Methodist Membership* Leader's Guide (no. M119B) and Member's Book (no. M120B).

2. *Living a New Life* (no. N105B).
3. *Getting the Story Straight* (no. N108B).
4. Pass-It-On-Books with titles such as: *How Can I Find God?, Who Is Jesus?, Why I Believe in the Church.*

To understand the distinctiveness of The United Methodist Church see:

1. *Beliefs of a United Methodist Christian*, Third Edition (no. DR025B).
2. *Four Great Emphases of United Methodism.* (no. M187K).
3. *Essential Beliefs for United Methodists* (no. M206K).
4. *My Membership Vows* (no. M269K).
5. *A New Adventure in the Meaning of United Methodist Membership.* Leader's Guide (no. M119B); Member's Book (no. M120B).
6. *The United Methodist Primer, Revised Edition* (no. DR024B).
7. *The United Methodist Member's Handbook* (no. M283K).
8. *United Methodist Doctrine* (no. DR080B).
9. *Scriptural Holiness* (no. DR053B).

To study our practice of the sacraments, see:

1. *Sunday Dinner: The Lord's Supper and the Christian Life* (no. UR429). Includes a study guide.
2. *Remember Who You Are: Baptism: A Model for Christian Life* (no. UR399).
3. *When United Methodists Baptize* tract (no. M198L).
4. *Our Sacraments* (no. M278K).
5. *When United Methodists Commune* tract (no. W150T).

To understand the history and practices of the congregation:

1. Have storytellers meet with the class to tell their stories (carefully prepared!).
2. Share a written history.
3. Tour the grounds and buildings, describing the significance of what you see.
4. Talk about typical worship services of the congregation, using printed orders of worship if available.
5. Have congregational leaders meet with the class to describe program and ministry areas.
6. Prepare a *brief* leaflet on the history of your congregation.

To help newcomers meet and develop friendships with other members:

1. Spend part of every meeting getting to know each other.
2. Plan a purely social time for the class.
3. Design classes that are not only lecture but also opportunities for class members to share their experiences and hopes.
4. Give the class the opportunity to continue as a class.
5. Help newcomers become part of an existing class or groups.

To help newcomers identify, claim, and begin to use their gifts, see:

1. *Gifts Discovery Workshop.* Leader's Guide (no. ST046K); My Giftbook (no. ST045K).
2. *Persons with Gifts to Share* (no. ST020B).
3. The worksheet in this booklet entitled "Identify, Claim, and Use Gifts."
4. *Time and Talent Inventory* (no. E244T).

To understand and begin to develop spiritual disciplines, see:

1. *Workbook of Living Prayer* (no. UR323).
2. *The Workbook on Spiritual Disciplines* (no. UR479).

A Meaningful Service of Reception

For most newcomers, joining a congregation is a significant event in their lives. The time in the service when they are formally received into membership is likely to be uncomfortable for most. However, this does not mean that the service of reception should be perfunctory or impersonal. Congregations will want this time to be remembered by newcomers as a special moment in which their faith commitments were acknowledged and celebrated and in which they heard the congregation's commitment to them verbalized.

People involved in the ministry of incorporating new members can work carefully with their congregation's pastor and worship committee to develop a service of reception that:

- Introduces newcomers in a personal way to the congregation;
- Shares with the congregation at least one of the reasons the person is joining;

- Indicates briefly what the congregation offers the new member and what the congregation expects from members;
- Provides a ritual in which newcomers and other members re-affirm their vows to God, to the church, and to each other.

Various United Methodist resources, including *The United Methodist Hymnal*, offer guidelines that can be used for the ritual part of the service of reception. Congregations currently not using these rituals will find that their use would enrich their worship experience. Congregations using the rituals may want to personalize them more by giving very direct attention to the new members and their individual reasons for joining.

To be sure, not everyone will want to make a personal statement during the service. After checking with the new member, a pastor or other appropriate person could share with the congregation one of the reasons the person is joining with a statement like: "John is joining us partly because he wants to participate in our ministry with street people." Or, "Maureen has found friends and support in our widows group and now wants to join us to continue her faith journey." Or, "Denise says that our sanctuary and worship service help her feel close to God."

Such short statements, whether made by the newcomers themselves or by church leaders, help the congregation know something about the newcomer and also help the congregation learn what is attracting newcomers. Furthermore, when attention is given to newcomers' reasons for joining, commitments can be made to help them continue their particular faith journeys.

Likewise, as the congregation voices its commitments to the newcomers, it can gently restate what the congregation expects from the newcomers. For example, a sentence or two about the expectations for prayers or presence or gifts or service could clarify for members and newcomers ways in which they can grow in these areas. This mutual commitment might be symbolized by having new members sign, during the service, the congregation's membership book.

The reception of new members must never be merely tacked on to the end of the worship service. Congregations which have new members joining often will devise ways to keep this part of their service fresh and invigorating. Other churches which receive new members only a few times a year can consider building their whole service around the reception of the new members.

What could be a more fitting climax to any worship service than a reception of new members that celebrates the commitments we make to God, to the church, and to each other?

STRATEGY III

Identify and Use Gifts

One of the primary ways we grow as disciples of Jesus the Christ is to identify our God-given gifts and to use them. Vital congregations understand that their purpose centers on helping people hear God's call to them and on helping them act on God's call. Clearly this was the pattern of care used by Jesus as he worked with the first disciples. He helped them recognize God's call; he trained them, sent them out to practice, helped them evaluate what happened, provided more training, and sent them out again. This continues as the purpose of the Body of Christ, the church. All of our people are our responsibility in this area, but often it will be our newest members who will be the most responsive to our efforts. When a congregation decides to begin a serious effort to help its people identify and use their gifts, it would do well to begin with its newer members. Many growing churches are consciously seeking to involve *each* member, new or old, in a ministry that fits a person's gift(s). Note carefully, the emphasis here is on people and their gifts, not on the institutional needs of a congregation.

Several excellent resources are available from Discipleship Resources to help people identify and claim their gifts and callings:

- *Gifts Discovery Workshop*
  Leader's Guide (no. ST046K); My Giftbook—1 for each participant (no. ST045K).

  A two-and-one-half hour workshop to help identify gifts and begin to see them in relationship with some of the needs of the community and world.

A more informal approach is to spend time with new members exploring questions, such as:

- Who are the three or four people you admire most? What have you done well? List ten things you like to do. How many are you doing now?

- When you consider others in your family, neighborhood, country and world, what is your gravest concern? What would you like to see done about your concern?

- What "gift" do you wish you had? Why? What area of ministry interests you most at this time?

As questions such as these are explored in counseling sessions or in small group discussions, many people develop a clearer understanding of their gifts and are encouraged to use and to develop their gifts.

DON'T FORGET

Every commitment to help people discover their gifts must be accompanied by a commitment to help them find a place of service in the church or in the larger community.

STRATEGY IV

Jobs, Roles, Leadership

Many people report that they felt they "belonged" to a congregation when they were given a job and felt they were needed. Other people drop away from congregations because they have felt pressured to accept responsibilities they either did not want or did not feel competent to undertake. Any committee charged with matching people and jobs will want to be very sensitive to the needs, concerns, and gifts of the people they are considering. The growth in discipleship of their fellow members will be their main concern rather than the filling of the job slots.

Also to be considered is the fact that people sometimes discover that they are, indeed, gifted as they dare to take on a new job or role in or through the congregation. Likewise, many firm friendships have been developed as people worked together toward a common goal.

The Institute for American Church Growth in Pasadena, California has determined that growing churches have sixty jobs or roles for every one hundred members. When a congregation has sixty responsibilities (legitimate jobs—committee member, teacher, choir member, circle leader, Boy Scout leader, etc.) for every 100 members, there will be few inactive members, and newcomers will soon find a place of service.

Effective Use of Gifts and Callings

Review Chapter Two to decide how your congregation accepts newcomers and integrates them into the life of the church. Your congregation will have a unique way of assigning responsibilities as you seek to provide every member with a specific ministry. Thus the person(s) who make these assignments will vary, but an effective use of the gifted persons in your congregation will require:

1. *Recruiting* people for jobs that match their identified or longed for gifts.
2. A *written job description* of the job which includes a timeline and expected results. They should participate in developing the description, and it should be kept simple.
3. Providing *adequate training* for every job, never assuming that a person already knows how the job is done. This maxim applies to the

most routine of tasks. Even people who have seen the offering collected thousands of times may not know what to do if asked to be collectors. A brief "walk through" may be all that's required, but those first steps make a difference in the experience of the nervous worker.

4. Building in mutual *evaluation times* when we call to ask how the job is going and to offer to help if things aren't going smoothly. These can also be times when people can admit that they made a mistake in accepting the job and that they wish to be relieved of their responsibility. If further training and assistance cannot insure that volunteers will have a positive experience, it may be best to allow (encourage) them to look for another place of service. Far too many people drop out of church because they accept jobs for which they have no gifts or to which they are not being called. They quickly burn out or become embarrassed because the job isn't being done or is not interesting. Sometimes the only way to be rid of the responsibility is to drop out! Our prayerful desire is to help the newcomer become an important part of the congregation, so honest, mutual evaluation is a vital skill to be cultivated.

5. *Thanking* people for their contributions. This simple courtesy is overlooked time after time in many congregations. We must not assume that people know we appreciate their efforts. In fact, they will assume we do not appreciate them unless we make it clear we do! One large "appreciation banquet" will not do the trick either. People need to be thanked personally and separately. Often a phone call, a short note, or brief public recognition is enough.

6. *Asking,* when one task is finished or a rest has been taken, *"What do you feel called toward now?"*

Some congregations have for each job or role a 4" x 6" card similar to:

Job/Role

People with compatible gifts:

_____

_____

_____

General job description (to be modified in consultation):

Training to be provided:

When a job or role has been accepted, the following 4″ x 6″ card is used:

	Job/Role
Person responsible	
Job Description:	
Training to be provided:	
	Date completed: _____

Check-ins	Date	Date	Date	Date
Results				

Formal "Thank you": _____ _____ _____
                              What   Who   Date

Leadership

Leadership functions in the church differ from leadership functions in the secular world. The business of the church is to enable the people inside the church as well as those outside the church to love God and neighbor more fully.

The question that church leaders ask first is "Where do we see God leading us?" The next questions are: "How can we help each other use our gifts and exercise our callings?" "How can we support and challenge each other?"

Churches that are serious about these questions will be careful to include newcomers in their leadership groups. Newcomers often are more familiar with community needs and concerns than are long-time members whose primary focus is the congregation's life. Newcomers can help congregations see where God may be leading the congregation, for they may be aware not only of community needs but also freshly tuned to the congregation's strengths. Their vision isn't so blurred by years of history and old assumptions.

Some congregations have decided that each of their church committees will have a minimum percentage of newcomers, if at all possible. Others have a policy of calling long-time members with job opportunities only after newcomers have been asked.

How do you include new members in your leadership circles? Many newcomers to our congregations will be receptive to accepting a job or a leadership role in our congregation. Several helpful resources on developing and using people in leadership roles in our congregations are available from Discipleship Resources, P.O. Box 189, Nashville, TN 37202 (615-340-7284):

1. *Seven Reasons to Volunteer in Our Church* (no. LA068K). Margie Morris gives scripturally based reasons for becoming an active participant in the ministries of the church.

2. *Job Descriptions for Local Church Leaders* (no. LD014M). A set of 36 8½" × 11" color-coded 2-page leaflets for the tasks and responsibilities in the Administrative Board or Council. Also includes the booklet, *Leaders Make a Difference.*

3. *Guidelines for Leadership in the Local Church: 1989-92* (set: no. 163870). This set of thirty booklets provides guidance for those persons

responsible for the administration and program of the local church. The booklets in this series are designed to help local church leaders identify their basic responsibilities and relationships, develop a plan for carrying out their work, and locate additional resources in all sizes and types of churches.

4. *Every Member in Ministry* (no. EV162K). John Ed Mathison gives practical suggestions on how to offer each member the chance to become involved in ministry.

STRATEGY V

Multiply Small Groups

It would be hard to overstate the importance of small groups in the life of all congregations. It must be noted here that single-cell churches are themselves small groups, albeit large small groups. These congregations which value, above all else, everyone knowing everyone resist mightily any attempts to divide their membership into smaller groups. Large groups in larger congregations may do likewise. Nevertheless, when a small membership church or any group grows beyond its capacity to care for newcomers, it must create new groups or cease growing. Small groups often can be a lifeline for people.

It is in small face-to-face, heart-to-heart groupings that we find the courage to talk about how we are experiencing God, or how we long to experience God. Often it is in small groups that we are challenged to take the next steps in our faith journey. Often it is in small groups that we find the love and support that sustains us in hard times.

Indeed, Warren Hartman, retired Research Director at the General Board of Discipleship, discovered a definite correlation between the number of adults involved in Sunday school classes and the number of adults who remain active in the life of the church. And the Institute for American Church Growth in Pasadena, California says that congregations need at least seven groups per hundred members.

Almost every congregation would be more effective in recruiting and incorporating new members if its small group life were more dynamic. Church growth research tells us that rarely is it possible for existing small groups to incorporate all newcomers. In fact, small groups tend to become essentially closed to new members. This is not the result of ill will or lack of concern. After a couple of years, small groups or classes usually have developed deep, meaningful relationships. The group will need to spend a great deal of energy maintaining those relationships. There isn't much time for newcomers. Furthermore, newcomers usually prefer to be part of new groups which they can shape to suit their needs and interests rather than to try to bend themselves into the mold of a long existing class or group.

Other factors also play a role. When a room is so full that newcomers cannot easily spot a seat, they will hesitate to enter. When a group has developed a very interactive, verbal style, newcomers may hesitate to join out of fear that they will be expected to speak up before they are ready. In short, successful long-term classes or small groups cannot be expected to meet the needs of newcomers. Churches do well to evaluate closely which of their current small groups may be "closed."

Class/ Group	Length of Existence	Room 85% Full?	Discussion or Lecture	Close Re- lationships	Open?/ Closed?

Concern for small group life leads to close working relationships with other committees. Are new Sunday school classes needed? New United Methodist Women's groups? What about a singles group? Or a new parents group? Or a "meals-on-wheels" group? A tutoring group? Or, a study on current issues group?

Don't be tempted to think that one group will meet everyone's needs or that every group will last forever. Once the need for a new class or group is uncovered, consider:

Steps in Beginning New Classes

1. Make a prospect list. List all members, especially new members, constituents, and prospects currently not in a group.

2. Talk with these people and analyze their needs, interests, concerns, and hopes. What would they like to do or study? What day and time is best for them? What else, such as child care, needs to be considered?

3. Call people together to discuss possibilities for new classes or groups. Make *personal* contacts through visits, calls, and letters, and use friendship networks to get people to come to the organizational meeting.

4. Decide what classes or groups are needed and can be supported. Usually a nucleus of five or six is plenty to get a new group started.

5. Set a time and place for the group(s) to begin meeting,

6. Help the group secure the best leadership available. Be flexible about methods of teaching and about frequency and length of meetings. New classes or groups often have better luck if the first teacher/leader is asked to serve on a temporary basis to help the group through the early stages of development.

7. Help the group choose curriculum.

Remember, not every new group will "make." Some will disband, but others will last and will be life-giving means of grace in the lives of members.

CLASS OR INTEREST GROUP			
Potential Members	Contacted by:	Date	Result

Exploratory Meeting _____
                              Date

Attendees:
_____
_____
_____
_____

Results: _____

Next Meeting: _____   _____
                        Time   Place
                   _____   _____
                     Leadership   Curriculum Materials

STRATEGY VI

Recordkeeping

Careful recordkeeping is important for every size congregation, but absolutely essential for mid- and large-size congregations that are serious about membership care. Small membership churches may hesitate at signing attendance pads or cards and suppose that they know exactly who is missing. This certainly will be true for all well-incorporated members, but the new member hanging around the fringes may not be missed at all. One congregation solved this dilemma by finding two long-time choir members to take turns keeping an attendance book. The membership was not disturbed, and the pastor had a definite record of attendance.

Large membership churches will do well to train the congregation to fill in attendance pads or cards every Sunday. People can understand their attendance as part of their spiritual discipline, and as part of their witness to, and support of, their neighbors.

Some congregations ask people to estimate their attendance rate for the year at the annual pledge time. When financial commitment reports are made, attendance reports are also made. Other congregations help members understand the importance of their presence by collecting attendance records along with the morning tithes and offerings. Most important, many congregations use the attendance pads to alert them to members whose attendance pattern is changing, who may be suffering in silence and isolation, or who may be drifting away from the congregation.

Frazer Memorial United Methodist Church in Montgomery, Alabama is such a congregation. The human warmth, concern, and response that have been generated by their recordkeeping system is astonishing. Frazer Memorial is one of the faster growing churches in our denomination, but it does not allow people to flow unnoticed from their front door out their back door. In 1985, at any given time, fewer than 10 percent of their members had been away from worship services more than three consecutive Sundays. This is a truly remarkable record.

Frazer Memorial uses the attendance pad available from Discipleship Resources (see sample sheet, p. 63). At every service people sign in. At the close of the services, volunteers collect the filled-in sheets and record the attendance of those present on cards (see the example on p. 64). Each family member's attendance is recorded with designated symbols in the

Our Worshiping Fellowship

That all of us here may know each other . . .

1. Please sign your name. Add phone and address if not a member here.

2. Pass this to your neighbor in the pew, last person in pew please return it to the starting point.

3. Upon its return, note the other names; you may meet a new friend in Christ today.

4. After the service, greet your neighbors and welcome our visitors.

(Check categories that apply)

NAME AND ADDRESS		Member of This Church	Attend But Not a Member	Visitor	New Resident	Desire a Call	Wish to Join This Church	Desire to Become a Christian	My Church Home (Name of Church, City, and State)
Name	Phone								
Address	Zip Code								
Name	Phone								
Address	Zip Code								
Name	Phone								
Address	Zip Code								
Name	Phone								
Address	Zip Code								
Name	Phone								
Address	Zip Code								
Name	Phone								
Address	Zip Code								

Turn to the next sheet when this one is full. Last person in pew please return sheet to starting point.

A003M

Discipleship Resources
P.O. Box 840, Nashville, Tenn. 37202

appropriate box. For example, the male adult is recorded by X, the adult female by +, and each child by √.

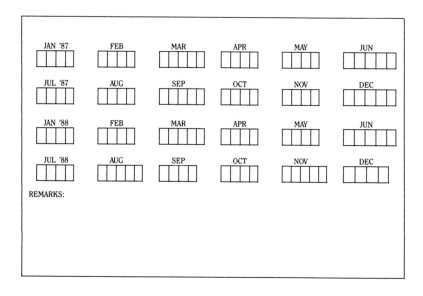

A core of volunteers makes the card entries on Sunday afternoon and Monday mornings. On Monday afternoons, other volunteers arrive to thumb through the cards and to flag any that show three or more consecutive absences. Those cards with seven or more absences receive a different color flag and are referred to pastors. On Tuesdays still more volunteers make telephone calls to those flagged. They call to say simply, "Hello, this is _____ from First United Methodist Church. We've been missing you (or someone in your family) at church and are calling to see if everything is alright with you."

This low-key, friendly call tells people they have been missed and obviously is very effective in keeping folks from drifting away from the congregation. Naturally, anything discovered by the telephone call that the staff of the church needs to know is reported. Consequently, the whole congregation's pastoral ministry is improved.

In this age of personal computers, someone in your congregation will be eager to computerize the information gained from attendance registration. It is hard to overstate the importance and effectiveness of such an intentional system for staying in loving contact with a congregation's membership. Further ideas about taking attendance during worship and follow-up with church members are found in *Taking Attendance* by Hoyt Hickman (Discipleship Resources, 1986; no. W121K).

TO BEGIN

1. Gain support and commitment from the congregation's decision-making body.

2. Explain the new system, stressing that its purpose is to stay in loving contact.

3. Recruit volunteers to:
   a. Record attendance.
   b. Check records for those whose attendance pattern is changing.
   c. Make friendly telephone calls on those who have been away for several weeks and report appropriately what they learn.

4. Work your plan consistently and faithfully.

The size of the congregation will determine the number of volunteers needed. Don't forget that the ministry of recording attendance can be managed by people who may be uncomfortable serving on committees or making more direct contact with people. Those who make the telephone calls can be people who are housebound. A ministry such as this can benefit many members!

STRATEGY VII

New Member Sponsors

Large membership churches report that one of their most effective ways of helping new members move into a complicated organization or situation is to find members who are willing to befriend them, introduce them to other members, help them find appropriate classes or groups, and help them find a place in the life and ministry of the congregation.

Each congregation will want to decide what will be accomplished by a new member sponsor program and then work backwards from that decision. One congregation gives the following job description to its members who agree to sponsor new members.

JOB DESCRIPTION FOR NEW MEMBER SPONSOR (MENTOR, FRIEND)

Our hope is that sponsors will befriend newcomers and help them move deeply into the life and ministry of our congregation. This process will take a minimum of three months. It will probably take longer. Our primary concern is that the newcomer's religious needs and belonging needs be met as fully as possible. Suggested activities include:

- Get acquainted with the newcomer before he/she joins.

- Give a packet describing church activities, group life, outreach ministries, etc.

- Attend worship services together—especially first few weeks.

- Monitor worship/Sunday school attendance; call after two or three consecutive absences.

- Learn interests, previous experiences in the church, hopes for participation.

- Invite for a meal.

- Introduce to other members.

- Help find a Sunday school class.

- Help find a small group—for study and for service (outreach project, choir, UMW, men's and women's Bible studies and discussion groups, committee work, etc.).

- Invite (pick up) to special activity (or find someone else to invite him/her).

- Report, *appropriately*, misunderstandings or disappointments experienced by newcomer.

- Make periodic reports to incorporation committee.

- Evaluate whole process at the end of the formal arrangement.

Some churches with a diverse membership or a large membership may discover they need a committee of people to recruit sponsors. No one knows a broad enough spectrum of the membership. Usually, newer, well-incorporated members make the best sponsors. Those recruiting sponsors will want to be especially aware of this group.

Like many other programs in the church, this ministry can be very effective and fruitful if it is carefully monitored, clearly explained to the participants, and if follow-through is consistent.

The number of expected newcomers will determine some organizational issues. If a church expects 20-30 new members a year, one coordinator, who knows the membership very well, may be able to recruit sponsors and monitor the developing relationships between the sponsors and the new members. Churches with more new members may need quarterly or monthly chairpersons.

EPILOGUE: THE FIRST YEAR

Intentionally helping newcomers move into the life and ministry of our congregations is not easy, but it is an essential task which is also an opportunity for the growth and joy of the newcomer and the congregation.

When we open ourselves and our congregations to strangers, when we share our faith journeys and are willing to hear their stories, we are Christ-like.

When we help others clarify their experiences of God and discern where God is calling them now, and when we allow them to challenge us to do likewise, we are Christ-like.

When together we worship and study, pray and accept our calling to reach out in love to God's world and children, then we are the Body of Christ.

Concern for newcomers can keep us alert to faith questions and fresh in our perspective on our communities. The effort to effectively incorporate new members is at the heart of the ministry of the church.

Have a joyful, blessed time as you open your hearts and congregations to newcomers, and do it during the first year.

Get $30.00 worth of books
FREE!

When you subscribe to the **Discipleship Resources Subscription Service** you receive **$60.00 worth** of books for your **$30.00** subscription price.
We will send you or your church organization from one to four brand new resources every other month for an entire year from the eight program sections of **The General Board of Discipleship.**
These resources (books, booklets, brochures, tracts, informational pieces, etc.) were written and produced solely to help the local church pastor and lay leaders in their ministries dealing with:

Evangelism
Christian Education
Worship
Stewardship
Ministry of the Laity
Ethnic Local Church
Concerns
United Methodist Men
Covenant Discipleship

Additional copies of resources that you find to be particularly helpful in your ministry can also be purchased with special subscriber coupons at **20% off** the regular price. What better/more inexpensive way is there to equip the leaders and committee members of your church with the tools they need to conduct their vital ministries in the name of Jesus Christ.

☐ **Yes, please enroll me for a one year subscription for just $30.00.**

Bill to: **Ship to:**
Name _____   **Name** _____
Address _____   **Address** _____
City/St/Zp _____   **City/St/Zp** _____

☐ **Payment enclosed**   ☐ **Bill me later**

Clip out this order blank and mail to:
DISCIPLESHIP RESOURCES, 1908 Grand Avenue, P.O. Box 189, Nashville, TN 37202
or call us at (615) 340-7284.